UNIVERSITY OF NORTH CAROLINA
STUDIES IN THE ROMANCE LANGUAGES AND LITERATURES
Number 42

RUTEBEUF AND LOUIS IX

RUTEBEUF AND LOUIS IX

BY

EDWARD BILLINGS HAM

CHAPEL HILL
THE UNIVERSITY OF NORTH CAROLINA PRESS

Depósito Legal: V. 2.859 — 1962

Printed in Spain - Talleres Tipográficos de la Editorial Castalia - Valencia, 1962

CONTENTS

	Page
I. POET AND KING	9
II. RENART LE BESTORNEI	35
TEXTUAL NOTES	45
ABBREVIATIONS	51

I

After the elaborate Faral-Bastin edition of Rutebeuf *(FB)*, it might be supposed that little more, if anything, need be said about the mysteries which have long obscured understanding of numerous elements in the attitudes of this singular thirteenth-century figure. *FB* has solved various problems with uncommon skill, but sundry questions still await convincing answers. Among these, a major example concerns Rutebeuf's several allusions to his king, Louis IX.[1] This problem is the subject of the present monograph.

For ground-work essential to this study, data already available must be reassembled and reordered. First, Rutebeuf's own verses relevant to Louis IX, and second, observations of twentieth-century scholars wherever useful. No adequate coördination of these data has been printed hitherto.

Some of Rutebeuf's references to the king involve conventional praise and pro-crusade clichés: *Complainte de Geoffroi de Sergines*, vv. 93-99; *Complainte d'outremer*, vv. 39-44, 73-81; *Complainte d'Eudes de Nevers*, vv. 121-129; *Voie de Tunis*, vv. 29-40; *Disputaison du croisé et du décroisé*, vv. 137-152. However, in this last passage (which Rutebeuf assigns to his *pro*-crusader) it may be useful to recall vv. 145-146 *(Moult a or meillor demoreir / Li rois vraiement que n'avons)* which, according to *FB*, suggest that Louis IX

---

[1] Earlier approaches of mine to this and to related topics: *Renart le Bestorné* (Ann Arbor [Michigan], 1947); articles in *Romance Philology* (IX [1955], pp. 133-138; XI [1958], pp. 226-239). Reviews of the 1947 monograph: Percival B. Fay, *RPh* I (1947), pp. 163-166; Alfred Ewert, *Medium Aevum* XVII (1948), pp. 54-55; Edmond Faral, *Romania* LXX (1948), pp. 257-269.

has more reason than his subjects for staying in France and for foregoing all further crusading.

A number of passages, written between 1257 and 1265, need more detailed attention:

Guillaume de Saint-Amour, *maître régent* of the theological faculty at the University of Paris, was banished from the city in 1257. This action immediately inspired the *Dit de Guillaume de Saint-Amour,* in which, as *FB* says, Rutebeuf "exhales his indignation" about broken promises wherein even the king was culpable. The poet refers (vv. 61-74) to an agreement involving the Mendicants and the university (cf. *FB* I, pp. 77-78): the latter's principal champion was Guillaume. Although the agreement was determined in the presence of the king and numerous witnesses, and although Louis IX gave assurance (vv. 81-84) that he would be the enemy of any violator, Rutebeuf asserts that Guillaume was then banished (either by the king or by Pope Alexander IV: cf. vv. 14-15) without any hearing (vv. 87-89: *Sanz ce que puis* [Guillaume] *ne mesfeïst / Ne la pais pas ne desfeïst, / Si* [le roi] *l'escilla sanz plus veoir*). Note that earlier in the poem Rutebeuf has these lines: *Qui escille homme sanz reson / Je di que Diex qui vit et regne / Le doit escillier de son regne* (vv. 6-8). And vv. 16-46 provide even more vehement excoriation:

Or vous dirai a briez paroles	16
Que, se l'apostoiles de Romme	
Puet escillier d'autrui terre homme,	
Li sires n'a nient en sa terre,	
Qui la verité veut enquerre.	20
Se li rois dit en tel maniere	
Qu'escillié l'ait par la prïere	
Qu'il ot de la pape Alixandre,	
Ci poëz novel droit aprendre,	24
Mes je ne sai comment a non,	
Qu'il n'est en loi ne en canon;	
Quar rois ne se doit pas mesfere,	
Por prïer c'on li sache fere.	28
Se li rois dist qu'escillié l'ait,	
Ci a tort et pechié et lait,	
Qu'il n'afiert a roi ne a conte —	32

S'il entent que droiture monte — 32
Qu'i[l] escille homme c'on ne voie
Que par droit escillier le doie;
Et se il autrement le fet,
Sachiez de voir qu'il se mesfet. 36
Se cil devant Dieu li demande,
Je ne respont pas de l'amande... 38
...Que ce soit sanz jugement 43
Qu'il sueffre cest escillement,
Je le vous moustre a iex voianz:
Ou droiz est tors et voirs noianz. 46

["Or, s'il y en a qui veulent savoir la vérité, je vous dirai en peu de mots que, si le pape de Rome est à même de décréter des exils de terres relevant d'autres seigneurs, ceux-ci ne peuvent rien dans leurs propres domaines. Si Louis IX prétend que c'est sur les instances du pape Alexandre IV qu'il a banni Guillaume, vous avez là l'occasion d'apprendre quelque chose de nouveau en fait de loi. Mais je ne sais pas le dénommer, parce qu'il ne se trouve rien de pareil ni en loi civile ni en droit canon; car roi ne doit pas méfaire, pour prière qu'on lui fasse. Si Louis IX dit qu'il a banni Guillaume, il est coupable d'injustice, de péché et d'outrage, parce que, à roi ou à comte qui tient à faire valoir la justice, il ne convient pas d'envoyer en exil qui que ce soit, à moins qu'il ne soit manifeste que cela se fait légalement: autrement, sachez bien qu'il s'agit d'un méfait. Si, devant Dieu, Guillaume demande réparation au roi, je ne réponds pas du châtiment qui pourra s'imposer... Que Guillaume soit condamné à cet exil sans connaissance de cause, je vous le prouve de toute évidence: la justice a été mise à l'envers et la vérité n'y est pour rien."]

While these lines were written as early as 1257 (a fact to be remembered *infra*), it became evident during the next two years that no one was going to help terminate Guillaume's exile and that he himself was not intending to repudiate principles in order to win release. And so Rutebeuf, in 1259, in the *Complainte de Guillaume* (vv. 174-179): *Ou a il nul si vaillant homme* [i. e., aussi courageux que Guillaume] / *Qui, por* [malgré] *l'apostoile de Romme* / *Ne por le roi,* / *Ne vout desreer son erroi* [changer sa conduite] / *De perdre honor*?

Faral (*FB* I, p. 285) interprets vv. 109-114 of the *Dit de Sainte Eglise* as follows: "Ah! si le Roi faisait sur ces gens-là [les Frères mendiants] une enquête qui fût aussi loyale que celle qu'il fait (*ou sur ces gens qui se prétendent si honnêtes une enquête comme il en fait*) sur les baillis! Que ne trouve-t-il, aussi bien, clerc ni prêtre qui ose enquêter sur leur comportement, de quoi le monde souffre tant!" The poem is preserved only in the poorest of the Rutebeuf manuscripts, but the textual difficulties do not give cause for misunderstanding the poet's feeling against the king.

An important passage in the bitterly sarcastic *Bataille des vices contre les vertus* (vv. 85-140) is probably best rendered through combination of *FB* (I, pp. 308-309) and Lucas:[2] "Plutôt que d'aller secourir l'empire latin de Constantinople (où les fous vont passer leur folie), ne vaut-il pas mieux faire enseigner humilité et sainte théologie dans un palais digne d'un roi, construit grâce à des aumônes, à des legs et à l'argent du meilleur roi [Louis IX] qui ait jamais détesté le désordre? Si l'Eglise peut excommunier, les Frères peuvent absoudre, à condition que les excommuniés soient à même de leur rendre la pareille. Pour mieux défendre Humilité si Orgueil voulait l'attaquer, les Frères ont fondé deux palais tels que, par la foi que je dois à l'âme de mon père, si Humilité y avait des provisions pendant huit ou neuf mois, elle s'inquiéterait fort peu d'Orgueil et de son *dangier* ['menace' (Lucas), 'pouvoir' *(FB)*]: au contraire, Humilité attendrait bien dans sa forteresse[3] qu'on vînt lui lever le siège. Certains médisants qui parcourent le pays prétendent maintenant que la mort du roi, à qui les Frères doivent leur honneur et leur prestige, changerait leur situation de fond en comble et diminuerait leur puissance. Tel qui leur fait bonne mine mépriserait leurs marques de faveur, et tel leur fait semblant d'amour qui ne le fait que de crainte. Je réponds... que leurs paroles sont vaines et frivoles. Si le roi... les comble de ses bienfaits et qu'ils en prennent, ils font bien, car ils ne savent pas combien ni quel temps cela peut durer... Ils

---

[2] *Rutebeuf—Poèmes concernant l'Université de Paris* (ed. Harry H. Lucas: Manchester and Paris, 1952), pp. 105-108.

[3] In v. 105 the reading of both manuscripts is *Ainz atendroit bien des le liege*. *FB* translates: "elle attendrait bien, depuis le pays de Liège", but what possible relevance can the Belgian city have in this context? The earlier editions of Rutebeuf prefer the common noun, for which Lucas suggests the plausible rendering "rempart".

savent bien à quoi s'en tenir... Voilà pourquoi ils fondent leur puissance sur des bases tellement solides, sachant parfaitement que, si leur puissance s'effondrait demain et si le roi mourait, ils auraient bien du mal à capitaliser les intérêts tels qu'ils se sont déjà machinés [*Que il avroient moult a fere / Ainz qu'il eüssent porchacié / Tel joiel comme il ont brassié*]."

Louis IX is the object of violent attacks in the *Ordres de Paris*. His gifts to the Sachets (a Mendicant order absorbed by the Augustinians in 1293) prompted Rutebeuf to say (vv. 80-84) that *Par un homme sont maintenu... Se mort le fet de vie nu, / Voisent la dont il sont venu, / Si voist chascuns a la charrue!* The poet goes on in similar vein about the Quinze-Vingts (vv. 85-96): *Li rois a mis en un repaire / (Mes je ne sai pas por qoi faire) / Trois cens avugles route a route* [ensemble]... *Si feus i prent, ce n'est pas doute / L'ordre sera brullee toute, / S'avra li rois plus a refaire*. But Rutebeuf is at his harshest in two stanzas (vv. 97-120) which presumably both refer to the order of the Filles-Dieu: "Des filles sont attribuées à Dieu, mais je n'ai jamais pu constater que Dieu ait eu femme en sa vie. Si vous tenez mensonge pour vérité et folie pour savoir, cela m'est égal. Je vous dis que ce n'est pas là un ordre religieux, mais plutôt fraude et supercherie pour jobarder les folles gens. On entre dans cet ordre aujourd'hui, on se marie demain: de même, le lignage de Notre Dame est plus nombreux aujourd'hui qu'il ne l'était hier. Le roi a des filles tellement à foison et il en a une si grande famille que personne n'aurait osé la prévoir. La France ne manque aucunement d'enfants: comme je prie Dieu de me garder en bonne santé, j'insiste qu'il n'est pas nécessaire de vendre des terres [comme les croisés, pour financer leur expédition] de crainte de ne pas pouvoir défendre la Terre Sainte, car le roi engendre des filles qui à leur tour en font autant. Les ordres glorifient le roi du nom d'Alexandre le Grand [à cause de sa largesse proverbiale], tant et si bien que, après qu'il sera devenuendre, ses éloges seront chantés pendant un siècle tout entier."

The twenty-line *Dit des Béguines* ends with a sharp thrust at Louis IX: "Si une Béguine se marie, c'est là son genre de vie; les vœux qu'elle prononce ne sont pas pour la vie. Cette année elle pleure et prie, l'année prochaine elle épousera un baron. Tantôt elle est Marthe, tantôt Marie; tantôt elle se refuse, tantôt elle se marie.

Mais n'en dites rien que du bien, car autrement le roi ne le supporterait point."

For completeness, a vague allusion may be recorded, from a poem which may not have been written by Rutebeuf (*Etat du monde*, vv. 159-160): "Nulle part au monde je ne vois ni prince ni roi qui se fasse scrupule de prendre" (Louis IX included here?). Although the *Dit d'Aristote* is a preachment against avarice (perhaps addressed to Philippe III), neither this poem nor the *Paix de Rutebeuf* seem to concern Louis IX: in any case, neither involves attitudes not already formulated by the poet elsewhere. Problems posed by the *Povreté Rutebeuf* are to be discussed in a separate paper.

A major commentary on Louis IX appears in the *Complainte de Constantinople* (vv. 133-168), but first, four earlier passages in this poem should be cited:

(1) "Île de Crète, île de Corse, île de Sicile, et Chypre (douce terre et douce île où il se trouvait du secours pour tous), quand vous serez sous la domination d'autrui, le roi de ce côté-ci de la mer convoquera une assemblée [sans doute celle du 10 avril, 1261] pour se rappeler comment Aiol[4] est venu en France. Et le roi fera construire de nouveaux établissements pour ceux [les Frères] qui sont les instaurateurs d'une nouvelle croyance, d'un nouveau Dieu et d'un nouvel Evangile [l'Evangile éternel]. Pusillanime, le roi laissera aussi Hypocrisie 'semer sa semence' dans cette ville de Paris où elle règne en souveraine" (vv. 37-48).

(2) *De la Terre Dieu qui empire, / Sire Diex, que porront or dire / Li rois et li quens* [son frère, Alphonse] *de Poitiers* (vv. 61-63)?

(3) *Or est en tribulacion / La terre de promission, / A pou de gent toute esbahie. / Sire Diex, por qoi l'oublion, / Quant por nostre redempcion / I fu la cha[i]r de Dieu trahie? / L'en lor envoia en aïe / Une gent despite et haïe, / Et ce fu lor destruction. / Du roi durent avoir lor vie; / Li rois ne l'a pas assouvie: / Or guerroient sa nascion* (vv. 85-96).

(4) *Or nous desfent on la carole, / Que c'est ce qui la terre afole, / Ce nous vuelent li Frere aprendre; / Mes Faussetez qui partout vole, / Qui Crestïens tient a escole* [tient sous sa férule], */ Fera la Sainte Terre rendre* (vv. 103-108).

---

[4] Cf. *Aiol, chanson de geste* (edd. J. Normand and G. Raynaud: Société des Anciens Textes Français, 1877).

The last two of these passages are readily translated, and yet the precise meaning of vv. 91-96 is still not clear. *Assouvie* 95 has been given various interpretations: "prise" (*FB* I, p. 423), "accomplie" (*FB* glossary), "mise à fin" (*PC,* p. 132), "Genüge getan" (Tobler-Lommatzsch I, 609). Only the last of these renderings seems admissible, particularly if the pronoun in v. 95 refers to *gent* 92, but the antecedents of the pronouns in vv. 91-95 are yet to be clearly identified. However, no matter the exact explanation of details in this passage, it is evident that Rutebeuf is reproaching Louis IX for remissness about the Holy Land.

For the important vv. 133-168 of the *Complainte de Constantinople,* the following interpretation is offered:

"Je ne vois pas comment on aimera Sainte Eglise, qui, de son côté, n'aime pas ceux auxquels elle est redevable de son prestige. Le roi méprise les chevaliers, bien que ce soit grâce à eux que Sainte Eglise se fait aimer. Toutefois, pour rendre droit et justice aux chevaliers, le roi s'en tient à les jeter — si haut placés qu'ils soient — l'un après l'autre dans des prisons fortes et redoutables. Plutôt que d'un Aymon de Bavière, le roi s'entoure d'une engeance hypocrite, vêtue de blanc et de gris [il s'agit des Frères Mendiants].

"Autant que ceci je fais savoir au roi: que, si le désordre venait à se déclarer en France, jamais pays ne serait aussi 'orphelin', car (ce serait un pays) où l'on aurait confié à la *gent beguine* [faux dévots] les armes, l'équipage militaire, la direction et toute la conduite des affaires. Alors on verrait les belles façons de ceux qui tiennent la France en leur possession, et qui ne connaissent ni règle ni mesure. Si les Tartares le savaient, jamais crainte de la mer [à traverser pour venir en France] ne les détournerait de telle entreprise de conquête.

"Tout en laissant les païens tranquilles, le roi se rend parfaitement compte de ce qui les retient: voilà pourquoi il tient son royaume de court,[5] si bien que tel est allé au pas qui se serait autrement élancé sur lui à bride abattue. Courte folie est plus saine que folie prolongée, celle-ci étant pleine de conseils idiots: or, que le roi reste maintenant chez lui, car, s'il n'avait pas exposé sa personne outre-mer [pendant la croisade de 1248-1254], le royaume s'en trouverait mieux aujourd'hui et le pays en serait plus à l'abri."

---

[5] Cf. *FSpec,* p. 330.

As indicated above, the passages introduced thus far were, in all probability, composed during the period 1257-1265. The most significant of all Rutebeuf criticism of Louis IX, however, appears in *Renart le Bestorné*. The date of this poem is a crux in Rutebeuf studies, and thereby of essential relevance for the poet's appraisal of his king. It is my belief that the poem postdates the latter's formal announcement (March 24, 1267; cf. *infra*) of taking the cross. More as appendix than otherwise, text and translation of *Renart le Bestorné*, with notes, are given in the second chapter of this monograph. Comment in the immediate pages which follow makes reference accordingly.

It is now time to sketch the essentials among twentieth-century opinions about Rutebeuf and Louis IX. Prior to 1946 (date of *PC*), the principal studies on Rutebeuf's ideas were those of Tiburtius Denkinger, Gerhard Feger, and Ulrich Leo, none of whom is mentioned [6] in *FB*.

Denkinger is less concerned with Louis IX than with the theory that Rutebeuf is intent above all on excoriating the Mendicant orders as hypocrites who, of course, hold complete sway over the king. It is the whole collection of hypocrites whom the fox personifies in *Renart le Bestorné*. Apparently unacquainted with Denkinger's work, Feger identifies the lion of the same poem with Philippe le Hardi, so that his observations about Louis IX in terms of other poems become little more than occasional paraphrase of Rutebeuf's own utterances. *Renart le Bestorné* is the primary topic in Leo's searching and extensive investigation, but the rest of the Rutebeuf repertory is also taken into serious account. As to the king, Leo is in essential agreement with Denkinger. In 1933, a brief article by Paul Keins [7] stressed the subservience of Louis IX to the Church as the real reason for Rutebeuf's Gallicanism: the king, however, is only an incidental factor in Keins's discussion.

---

[6] Except for a casual criticism of Denkinger's discussion of *Renart le Bestorné*, in *Franziskanische Studien* II (1915), pp. 97-102. Feger's *Rutebeufs Kritik an den Zuständen seiner Zeit* was published at Freiburg-in-Baden in 1920, and Leo's *Studien zu Rutebeuf* (Halle, 1922) is Beiheft 67 in the series sponsored by the *Zeitschrift für Romanische Philologie*.

[7] "Rutebeufs Weltanschauung im Spiegel seiner Zeit", in *Zeitschrift für Romanische Philologie* LIII, pp. 569-575.

Most of the historical commentary in *PC* and in *FRom* is kept intact in *FB,* so that Faral's final views about Rutebeuf and the king are drawn from the latter.[8] These opinions, as set forth in *FB* I, pp. 47-49, require review and reappraisal here. Accordingly, the following excerpts (suspension-points not necessary):

"En tant qu'elles concernent les questions politiques et religieuses, les idées de Rutebeuf ont eu pour principe animateur (1255-1270) son hostilité à l'égard des Ordres mendiants. De là, son attitude à l'égard du roi, qu'il n'a guère aimé et dont il lui est arrivé de parler avec une audace frisant le défi. Déjà en 1257, à propos de Guillaume de Saint-Amour, il l'accuse hardiment ou bien de n'avoir pas su défendre ses droits souverains contre le pape, ou bien de s'être exposé au châtiment de Dieu pour avoir manqué à la justice. Plus tard, il raille le pullulement [des Ordres mendiants] vivant de la mendicité et dont le roi était l'inépuisable bienfaiteur. Il l'a appelé en passant, dans la *Bataille des Vices contre les Vertus,* le 'meillor roi qu'onques encor haïst desroi'. Mais ce n'a été que pour supputer un peu plus loin (qui sait avec quelle secrète espérance?) ce qu'il adviendrait des Jacobins et de leurs orgueilleuses constructions 'se Diex avoit le roi pris, par qui il ont honor et pris': idée qui reparaît dans les *Ordres de Paris,* pièce où se lisent trois vers [118-120] d'une cruelle ironie sur la gloire qui l'attendra 'après ce qu'il sera cendre'. Fidèle à l'idée d'entreprises auxquelles, en toute occasion pendant vingt ans, [Rutebeuf] a toujours poussé, il ne pouvait, en 1267 [cf. *La Voie de Tunis*], refuser son éloge au roi qui venait de se croiser. Mais [comme dans la *Complainte de Constantinople*] l'approbation ne venait que dans la mesure où le roi parait au péril créé par l'ingérence des Jacobins dans sa politique. Dans *Renart le Bestourné,* la critique atteint son paroxysme: une critique indignée, celle d'un homme atteint en ses intérêts matériels les plus directs, privés de ce que les 'bonnes festes' lui apportaient de profit. [De] terribles paroles [vv. 155-162] ne sont dardées contre le roi que parce qu'il n'a d'oreilles que pour les Frères, qui se sont emparés de

---

[8] Pertinent passages about the king occur in Vol. I, pp. 47-49, 51, 53, 56-57, 70-71, 74, 78-81, 82-93 (a section devoted primarily to the crusades, 1254-1281), 304, 318-321, 327, 372, 520, 559, 565-566, 569-570; and in Vol. II, pp. 175-176.

son esprit et qui, avec quelques autres, sont devenus les maîtres de son hôtel."

In the commentary (*FB* I, pp. 533-536) which accompanies the text of *Renart le Bestorné*, Faral maintains essentially the views which he advanced in 1948 *(FRom)*, and with virtually the same firmness of conviction. Salient observations are as follows: "La mention de Constantinople [vv. 14-21] n'a rien à voir avec l'histoire de la chute de cette capitale, rien dans le texte n'éveille l'idée d'une croisade, et par conséquent tout essai pour identifier des personnages en partant de cette idée, voué d'avance à un échec, ne peut avoir de meilleurs résultats que les suppositions anciennes et gratuites de Jubinal. Le *fait certain* [italics mine] est qu'on ne saurait songer à des seigneurs ou à des chevaliers, puisque l'idée d'un rôle joué à la guerre par ses quatre personnages [Renart, Isengrin, Roniel, Bernart] a été présenté par l'auteur comme une absurdité. Des noms pourraient être avancés, sans qu'aucun puisse l'être avec certitude, ni même avec probabilité. Mais il n'en reste pas moins qu'il s'agit de personnages en service à l'Hôtel du Roi. Le sens du poème étant défini comme nous l'avons fait, la date de composition en serait l'année 1261." [9]

The principal modification in Faral's position since 1948 involves his virtual abandonment of attempts to identify the animal-personages, but also an explicit insistence that none can be knight or noble: however, while possibly true, this is neither proved nor provable. At the same time, Faral is on sound ground in urging that *Renart le Bestorné* was motivated by a specific event ("fait certain, fait du jour, actualité"), an event occurring after 1254 when the king returned from his first crusade and before his death in 1270. There is full agreement that the relevant occurrence is to be searched out among the following:

(1) The Paris assembly of April 10, 1261, when austerity measures (cf. *FB* I, pp. 532-533) were proclaimed at the court, depriving numerous individuals of cherished privileges.

(2) The Greek recapture of Constantinople, July 25, 1261.

---

[9] But cf. *FB* I, p. 48, where Faral mentions 1262 as the date for the *Complainte de Constantinople*, and refers to *Renart le Bestorné* as "écrit peu de temps après".

(3) The Paris assembly of March 24, 1267, when Louis IX accepted the crusader's cross from the Franciscan cardinal of St. Cecilia (Simon de Brion, later Pope Martin IV [1281-1285]).

(4) The treaty of Viterbo (May, 1267) which, for all practical purposes, made the king's brother, Charles of Anjou, heir to the unregained throne in Constantinople.

(5) Increasingly sharp and widespread criticism of the Mendicant Orders during the 1260's: obviously, to be sure, this is trend rather than isolated event.

(6) The Tunis crusade, summer of 1270. This expedition had been pushed by Charles of Anjou, although, as Fay suggests (cf. *RPh* I, pp. 165-166), he may have regarded it as only the least bad substitute — or preliminary — for a direct move to retake Constantinople.

Faral lays *Renart le Bestorné* to the austerity measures promulgated in 1261 and to the "verve vengeresse" which thereupon animated Rutebeuf. The editor's view is supported by vv. 141-147, which may indeed include an excoriation of the 1261 decrees. However, a number of considerations raise serious doubts. For example, Rutebeuf nowhere claims that he himself ever had personal access to the court, far less that he himself was among those excluded by new rulings. Furthermore, his criticisms in the *Dit de Sainte Eglise* and in the two poems about Guillaume de Saint-Amour show that his dislike for Louis IX antedates the 1261 assembly by at least four years and, as early as 1257, had carried him even to the point of spelling out a charge of mendacity: it is scarcely likely that Rutebeuf's participation in court affairs was being encouraged thereafter, whatever his standing (if any) prior to Guillaume's exile from Paris. Also it is equally — and perhaps even more — significant that nowhere else in the Rutebeuf repertory is there a single passage where injustice or affront to himself personally is brought forward as basis for an attack against the king or, for that matter, against anyone else. Finally, Faral himself points out (*FB* I, p. 534) that "les jongleurs ont toujours protesté contre les dîners 'à porte fermée'" and then goes on to cite examples (some of them well before 1261) which reduce the thought in *Renart le Bestorné* 141-147 virtually to the level of thirteenth-century cliché. Why then, failing any reasonable alternative, rely on such scant evidence of motivation to account for Rutebeuf's poem?

Within three months after the April assembly in Paris, the Greeks reëntered Constantinople, overthrew the emperor Baldwin II, and thus ended more than a half-century of French rule. Is it conceivable that any French writer in the 1260's, remembering that the *Roman de Renart* (branch XI) recounts an attempt by the fox to dethrone King Noble (whose very capital is Constantinople), would be either unaware or unmindful of this rather recent disaster for the French at Byzantium? Yet, with no supporting evidence or reasons, Faral has stated categorically (cf. *supra*) that in *Renart le Bestorné* vv. 14-21 (cf. *infra* for note on this passage) have nothing to do with the fall of Baldwin II!

Neither in *FRom* nor in *FB* does Faral mention — in connection with *Renart le Bestorné* — the king's formal act [10] of taking the cross in 1267, a further circumstance which gravely jeopardizes the theory that the poem was written earlier in the decade. The accent on military danger is so pronounced in *Renart le Bestorné* that it is difficult to believe that the poem's few lines of vehement cliché about court festivities are more than a conveniently parenthetical whip-lash to reënforce more serious preoccupations. In any case, for the record as Rutebeuf wanted it known, *Renart le Bestorné* is aimed at a national policy of immeasurably greater concern to the poet's hearers and readers than any social-hour resentments of a mere individual.

Divergent opinions during the past fifteen or twenty years call for restatement and elaboration of the position that *Renart le Bestorné* was written after Louis IX took the cross in 1267, that it was conceived in protest against the projected venture which ended in the Tunis tragedy of 1270, and that it was above all a magnification of Rutebeuf's long-standing repugnance concerning royal policies and counselors. Precisely with the help of Faral's constructively detailed argumentation in *FRom* and *FB*, the poem fits chronologically more and more naturally into a brief period after the 1267 Paris assembly and the Viterbo treaty. However, it should be interpolated here that, since my interpretation of Rutebeuf's feelings about crusade enterprises in the thirteenth century has been already intimated (*RPh* XI, pp. 234-239), I need only repeat the conclusion

---

[10] This act is, however, mentioned (*FB* I, p. 461) in his convincing discussion of the date of the *Voie de Tunis*.

that, while he may have been commercialized for propaganda purposes by this person or that, he was rarely (if ever) more than a half-hearted believer in the usefulness of late thirteenth-century Holy Land activity. Numerous passages in the allegedly pro-crusade poems support this view, notably including even the occasional moments when Rutebeuf has a mildly good word for Louis IX.

In *Renart le Bestorné* the emphasis on military danger is unmistakable, and it is particularly explicit in vv. 14-21, 28-30, 86-103, 161-162. All the rest of the poem supplies the reasons for this danger: the king's avarice, his political ineptitude, his self-serving counselors, and their preposterous incapacity for war. As for the specific war which Rutebeuf has in mind, the forthcoming 1270 crusade is the one and only possibility. Between 1254 and 1270 there is nothing else in the record of history to suggest military threat to France, except, of course, the remote Tartar menace to the Holy Land which helped to occasion the Paris assembly of 1261. But even Louis IX, dedicated as he was to crusading idealism, did not take the cross until six years later. The Tartars of the early 1260's simply did not provide sufficient justification.

Faral's comments on the significant v. 28 are cited *infra* in a note about this line. Here, however, it is essential to recall that, just as Rutebeuf considered that Renart might well seek out and find occasion to precipitate a war, so also vv. 91-109 foretell explicitly and with violent ridicule the débâcle to come in case he did. Also, history has long since shown that the Tunis sidetracking of the 1270 crusade proved to be much more of a calamity than anything even in Rutebeuf's dismal prognostic in the closing lines of *Renart le Bestorné*.

At this point, it is useful to examine a parallel (and supporting) distribution of emphasis in the poem. Vv. 1-27 (i. e., exactly the first sixth of Rutebeuf's text) point up the perpetually self-renewing power of corruption which Renart is meant to symbolize; they show how *renardie* has deprived France of its kingdom in thirteenth-century Turkey and Greece; and they clearly label Renart as master of all royal *avoir* in France. The poet's immediate thought from v. 28 on is that, through willfully contrived involvement in war, Renart is in a fair way to ruin France with a tragedy for which Louis IX can blame only his unseeing faith in the cynical incompetents of the inner circle around him. Faral would have it that these incompetents can be only bureaucrats assigned to monetary and other routine concerns of the royal court, but Rutebeuf's anguish about imminent (yet needless) war surely refers to counselors at higher levels of national policy. Counselors who, in point of fact, whether for selfish reasons of their own or for misguided but honest hope about their king, were in a position to confuse or second his obvious yearnings to retrieve the crusade disaster of 1248-1254 in terms of one more gallant attempt to regain the Holy Land for Christendom. Rutebeuf never openly questioned the personal crusading aspirations of Louis IX, but, in a manner far less mild than Joinville's, he made it abundantly clear in *Renart le Bestorné* that his king should have had the elementary intelligence to see that the days for Holy Land traffic (by warfare from western Europe) were ended.

About a fifth of the poem stresses the king's avarice and its effects; vv. 84-106 return to the theme of vv. 28-30, with renewed emphasis on his lack of either loyal or competent supporters in the event of war; Rutebeuf devotes the final third to the grim hopelessness of this prospect for Louis IX. Or, in other words, at least thirty verses (28-30, 84-103, 155-162) discuss explicitly military danger, and everything else in *Renart le Bestorné* bears consistently and unequivocally upon this preoccupation of the poet.

As previously seen here, Faral takes it virtually for granted that Rutebeuf's political and religious views have as their "principe animateur" his hatred of the Mendicants, and that this accounts for his dislike of Louis IX. Is this necessarily the case? Only two of Rutebeuf's extant poems about the friars are known to antedate the banishment of Guillaume de Saint-Amour (August, 1257). The first of these, *Le Dit des Cordeliers,* is *favorable* to the Franciscans. The second, *La Discorde de l'Université et des Jacobins,* attacks the Dominicans for attempting to acquire faculty appointments in the University of Paris. Moreover, this poem is a kind of sequel, supporting an anti-Dominican manifesto instigated presumably by Guillaume in 1254 (cf. *FB* I, pp. 70-71). In other words, Rutebeuf's first known expression of criticism about the Mendicants arises in connection with his espousal of the established faculty's cause in the university quarrel and with his devotion to Guillaume.

From 1254 on, Rutebeuf is particularly bitter against the Mendicants for machinations involving university affairs and crusade policies. Perhaps he would have levelled diatribes at the friars even if they had been on the "right" side in both these areas. Perhaps he would have disliked them regardless. But can it not be suggested that Rutebeuf was first moved to wrath by loyalty to Guillaume and the university and only then, in corollary fashion, by what he came to despise on the part of both friars and king? And similarly in relation to crusades? Can it not be said that Rutebeuf's positive concern *for* the university cause and *for* the national safety was at least as deeply felt as his negative regarding the Mendicants? Definitive answers, either way, are not demonstrable. At the same time, Faral's view is supported by the historical fact of the king's sympathies with the Mendicants and by Rutebeuf's several passages asserting the king's subservience to these orders. But, despite cursory reference to Joinville (ed. de Wailly, ch. 142: cf. *FB* I, pp. 319-320), Faral omits any mention of the chronicler's views as they apply to issues under review here. Consequently, the record must be made complete.

In chapters 139, 142, 143, Joinville shows that the charities of Louis IX embraced far more beneficiaries than just the Mendicant Orders. The chronicler notes that some of the king's "familiers groussoient de ce que il fesoit si larges aumosnes", but adds — almost as if to refute Rutebeuf himself — that "ja pour les grans despens que li roys fesoit en aumosne ne lessoit il pas a faire grans despens en son hostel chascun jour... et fesoit servir si courtoisement a sa court, et largement et habandonnement, et plus que il n'i avoit eu lonc temps passei a la court de ses devanciers."

Except for possible oversight on my part, *FB* contains no hint of the following criticism of the Tunis crusade (Joinville, ch. 144): "Je entendi que tuit cil firent pechié mortel qui li [Louis IX] loerent l'alee, pour ce que ou point que il estoit en France, touz li royaumes estoit en bone paiz en li meismes et a touz ses voisins; ne onques puis que il en parti, li estaz dou royaume ne fist que empirier. Grant pechié firent cil qui li loerent l'alee, a la grant flebesce la ou ses cors estoit... Et si, febles comme il estoit, se il fust demourez en France, peust il encore avoir vescu assez, et fait mout de biens et de bonnes oeuvres."

While Joinville does not identify any of those who were urging the king to undertake the 1270 crusade, neither does he at any point set down adverse criticism of any religious order. But, while often seeking guidance from counselors, Louis IX did not hesitate to take a contrary course (cf. Joinville, [e. g.] ch. 135). About subservience either to individuals or to organized groups, it must be remembered that obviouly Joinville was a friendly critic, whereas Rutebeuf was not. It must also be remembered that, equally obviously, Rutebeuf may have thought it strategically advantageous simply to charge the king with subservience whenever the latter elected to follow a "wrong" course. Therefore, to conclude that Rutebeuf's vehemence against the Mendicants automatically explains his attacks on the king is less than justified.

* * *

In *FRom* Faral was saying back in 1948 that the animals in *Renart le Bestorné* could be identified in a score of different ways, each in effect as worthless as every other, and in *FB*, as noted *supra*, he gave up the problem altogether. That twenty sets of identifications might be improvised (with due allowance for Faral's "twenty" as being intentionally rhetorical rather than realistic) is out of the question, on account of the known circumstance that the intimates of Louis IX were remarkably few in number. If the poem were prompted by the assembly of 1261, its accent on the danger of war could apply only to the possible threat from the *gent tartarine* (cf. *Complainte de Constantinople*, v. 154), in which case machinations among the French king's alleged manipulators would hardly be an issue. On the other hand, after he took the cross in 1267, the prospect of graver military crisis comes into clearest focus for all to see. Consequently, with more confidence on my part than hitherto, my identifications for the principal animals in *Renart le Bestorné* remain reasonable. However, beyond the fact that each animal must represent *somebody*, it must be remembered that outright proof is still lacking, and no doubt always will be. At the same time, it must also be remembered that the poem was completely intelligible for its readers and hearers of seven centuries ago, and that its animal-characters were readily recognized. And what characters more obvious than those who, in Rutebeuf's mind, stood to profit each in his own way from the king's fanatical obsession with the crusade objective? The *dramatis personae* in *Renart le Bestorné* thus leave little room for choice.

It is well known that Charles of Anjou forwarded a long-standing ambition by way of the treaty of Viterbo and that he was one of the leading abettors of the 1270 crusade, in which, furthermore, an active part was played by his son, the future Charles II of Naples. The personal and political reputation of Charles of Anjou naturally lent itself most easily to a Renart fable designed in a spirit of hostile criticism. So why not nominate the father and son for the rôles of Renart and Grimaut?

However, about this choice of Charles of Anjou three queries need to be reviewed, the first two suggested by Professor Foulet in correspondence and the third by Faral in *FB* (I, pp. 534-535). It could be argued that, since *Renart le Bestorné* mentions no kinship between Renart and Noble, the author did not want these two animals to be recognized as brothers. In fact, beast-epic tradition would prevent them from being regarded as such, even in so casual an appropriation of earlier legend as *Renart le Bestorné*. At the same time, this very circumstance would only make it easier for a momentarily discreet Rutebeuf to shield his attack on Charles of Anjou by deliberate omission of any direct statement about his blood relationship to the king of France. In other words, the most natural interpretation virtually requires the assumption that the poet purposely avoided any such obvious link between lion and fox. If anything, therefore, the negative evidence in this connection seems only to strengthen the case for identification of Renart with the brother of Louis IX.

The second and perhaps the most serious question about Charles of Anjou as Renart ties in with the poet's remarks (vv. 46-48) charging Darius with avarice. As recounted in the *Roman d'Alexandre*,[11] however, the Persian king was not killed because of avarice but because he had antagonized his *gentieus homes*. Not that this discrepancy in *Renart le Bestorné* matters: Rutebeuf is interested only in the point that the way of royal avarice is a way of royal disaster. While the internal troubles which Darius had created for himself facilitated Alexander's invasion success, Rutebeuf gives no inkling that he anticipates any attack from a nation

---

[11] Cf. *The Medieval French 'Roman d'Alexandre'*, vol. II (edd. Edward C. Armstrong et al.: Princeton and Paris, 1937), p. 148. This, the essential reference, is not included in *FB* (I, p. 540 [note 46]).

outside. Yet if he were in fact thinking of some such vague onslaught, it could be supposed that he viewed the corruption in France as a form of *renardie* which would expose the nation to inevitable blows from watchful foreigners. And if such was his purpose in writing *Renart le Bestorné*, it would not necessarily follow that the fox should be identified with Charles of Anjou. But in v. 28 the poet says that *Renars porra mouvoir teil gueirre*, which surely means that Renart is interested in taking some sort of military initiative. Rutebeuf apparently regards Renart as too skilled an intriguer ever to expose his own points of vantage to anything as harmful as an uninvited conflict with another nation. If this interpretation is not valid, it is reasonable to suppose that, even in a poem of veiled hints, the Darius allusion would have included something about Alexander's invasion. Moreover, the reference to the ounce (vv. 155-157) implies that the opponents of Renart would prefer hostile incursion from outside as against the risks which the fox is aggravating from within.

In *FRom* (p. 265) Faral stated categorically that Renart "est représenté [dans *Renart le Bestorné*] comme le sont ailleurs, chez Rutebeuf, les Frères Mendiants et, spécialement, les Jacobins... On notera que les vers 25-27 peuvent signifier qu'il s'agit d'une collectivité. S'il est dit que Renart a un fils nommé Grimaud (v. 131), c'est peut-être un trait contre les Cordeliers." Wisely, Faral does not return in *FB* to this suggestion about Grimaut. But his reasons for associating Renart with the Mendicants want quotation in full (*FB* I, pp. 534-535): Renart "est, dans le roman de son nom, le symbole de la ruse et de l'astuce; mais en beaucoup d'autres poèmes, il est celui de l'hypocrisie religieuse. Rutebeuf lui-même, dans la *Discorde de l'Université* (v. 53-54), l'a imaginé ceint de la corde et vêtu de la cotelle des Cordeliers; il a, dans le *Pharisien* (v. 80-86), représenté 'Ypocrisie la renarde' venant au royaume de France en la personne des Frères; il a, dans les *Règles* (v. 8 ss.), comparé les procédés des Jacobins à certaines ruses du renard pour prendre les oiseaux. De même, dans notre poème, ce sont les Frères qu'en la personne de Renart il met en cause. On en a une *preuve* [italics mine] aux vers 85-103, où il se gausse de l'idée bouffonne d'une armée qui, en cas de besoin, serait conduite par Renart, Ronel, Isengrin et Bernart: car, dans la *Complainte de Constantinople* (v. 145-156 [cf. *supra*]), blâmant le roi de rabaisser ses chevaliers, il a de même évoqué le spectacle dérisoire d'une armée formée à leur place par la 'gent béguine', expression qui, selon le contexte, désigne à la fois les Frères et leurs tenants. L'idée domine donc, dans notre poème, d'inspirations venues des Frères et exerçant leurs maléfices sur l'esprit du roi."

Thus, in Faral's own words, his thesis stands or falls by his conviction that Louis IX is the pliable and ever-willing victim of Mendicant "maléfices": the inadequacy of this view has been pointed out *supra*. But, what of the four supporting passages which Faral invokes? In the *Discorde de l'Université* Rutebeuf says merely that the Franciscan habit, if resorted to by Renart, will not improve his foul way of life: there is no hint of personification. The *Pharisien* passage does no more about the fox than equip Hypocrisy with the adjective *renarde*. In *Des Règles* there is again no hint of personification: vv. 8-15 only compare Dominican deception with the trickery in an early episode in the *Roman de Renart*. The fox is not even mentioned in the *Complainte de Constantinople*: nor does any passage in this poem either prove or disprove anything about *Renart le Bestorné*. Finally, in saying that Renart *has* an extensive *norreture*, v. 25 hardly personifies Renart himself as any "collectivity".

As for the lesser animals in the poem, the most reasonable identifications are the following. The devious, calculating, and rarely belligerent Jean le Roux of Brittany, who played a large part in the Tunis crusade, would fit Ysengrin; while his son, the future duke Jean II, who was also in the crusade, would fit Primaut.[12] Bernart "with his cross" could well be the Franciscan Eudes Rigaud, archbishop of Rouen, who was the principal ecclesiastical participant in the crusade. Roniel the dog could be the youthful and eager Thibaut II of Navarre and Champagne who, among other things, shared in the famous failure to persuade Joinville to engage in the ill-fated expedition.

Jean le Roux was duke of Brittany for nearly half a century 1237-1286), a period during which the Tunis crusade was his only military activity of consequence.[13] It is recorded that on the cru-

---

[12] In the *Roman de Renart*, however, Primaut is Ysengrin's brother, and not his son as in *Renart le Bestorné* (vv. 128-130).

[13] Cf. Arthur Le Moyne de La Borderie, *Histoire de Bretagne* (Rennes, 1906), III, pp. 343, 352-353.

sade he was accompanied by his wife, son, and daughter-in-law; that he invested 87,000 livres in the venture; that several Breton vassals went along with him. After the king's death Jean le Roux returned to Brittany, while his son continued to Syria and did not come back to Europe for another two or three years. La Borderie (*op. cit.*, p. 335) describes Jean le Roux as consumed with ambition, with "ardeurs autoritaires", with "convoitises de pouvoir personnel", with "passion thésaurisante". He was "prudent, méfiant, calme, impassible en apparence, mais avec une obstination tenace et une suite dans ses projets que [son] père n'avait pas... rentrant ses griffes, tapi dans un coin, attendant et attirant à lui patiemment, sûrement, la proie convoitée, au lieu de bondir sur elle — et de la manquer... Il visait avant tout au solide, à arrondir ses domaines et remplir ses coffres, voyant là la base la plus certaine de sa puissance." It is easy to imagine that a hostile critic could accuse such a personage of readiness to run from battle at the crucial moment.

As for Eudes Rigaud, it should be remembered here that he was one of a commission of four which, in 1256, drew up a solution of the quarrel between the Mendicants and the University of Paris: a solution which in effect satisfied nobody.[14] Thus it is not hard to charge the author of *Renart le Bertorné* with irritation at the archbishop's prominent rôle in the projected crusade. Furthermore, since leaders who actually participated in the venture would be the most likely targets for criticism by its opponents, what is more reasonable than to identify Bernart with the most conspicuous ecclesiastic in the 1270 retitnue of Louis IX, especially with one so high in the Franciscan hierarchy (regardless of Eudes Rigaud's enviable reputation in recorded history)?

Despite the zealous activities of Thibaut II of Navarre, identification of him with Roniel can be at best only a guess. Just possibly, incidentally, Rutebeuf was using the dog for an extra touch of irony, since in Church iconography this animal symbolizes such qualities as faithfulness, orthodoxy, loyalty to a sovereign.

Other possibilities have been suggested as identification for the personages attacked in *Renart le Bestorné*, notably (but not with conviction) by Faral, in *FB* (I, p. 536) and in *FRom* (pp. 264-265).

---

[14] Cf. M.-D. Chapotin, *Histoire des Dominicains de la Province de France* (Rouen, 1898), pp. 450-453. Also *Leo*, p. 66 (note 43).

In addition, even Simon de Brion remains as a conceivable candidate, but he did not go on the crusade in 1270. Also, one of the animals might be linked with Pierre le Chambellan, a favorite minister of Louis IX for two decades after 1250 and a member of the expedition to Tunis. Two further participants who might be considered were the king's Dominican confessor, Geoffroi de Beaulieu, and his Dominican chaplain, Guillaume de Chartres. But none of the individuals mentioned in this paragraph or by Faral are vivid enough in the historical record of the crusade to demand more than passing reference in any study of *Renart le Bestorné*, and there are no other important figures known to have been seriously influential in the final years of the reign. Lastly, and in any event, it should again be stressed that the most likely identifications will always be limited to principals who actually took part in the quixotic detour to Tunis.

The principal *Renart le Bestorné* question which remains for discussion here is that of the mystification by way of animal disguisings. While it is well known historically that before its inception the 1270 crusade encountered vigorous opposition in France, it is more important in relation to the poem to remember that the formal blessing accorded the venture by Pope Clement IV was heavy with doubt and reservation: even Wallon [15] admits that only the exceptional fervor of Louis IX induced the pope to give the crusade any endorsement at all. Under such circumstances, perhaps the lay poet of *Renart le Bestorné* found caution to be the better part of valor. Also, in at least three poems Rutebeuf would be formulating high praise for both Thibaut of Navarre and Charles of Anjou (cf. *FB* I, pp. 431-439, 479-485). And he is credited with a *Voie de Tunis* in support of the very crusade which it is here proposed to have *Renart le Bestorné* condemn. In the latter poem, then, what further reason for mystification?

Since there is no mention of Tunis in the *Voie de Tunis* poem except in the rubric, its title was presumably introduced by some later scribe who was recording texts quite arbitrarily under a convenient Rutebeuf rubric, and who had no preoccupation with accuracy. Incidentally, the *Voie de Tunis* was obviously written before the crusade, while its title equally obviously postdates the side-

---

[15] H.-A. Wallon, *Saint Louis et son temps* (Paris, 1876), II, p. 422.

tracking to North Africa (cf. *FB* I, p. 461). The poem is a dull business in which the reader is asked to view the projected expedition not only with sympathy, but also with willingness to enter in as a participant. Since it was not known until the last minute that the French were going to make Tunis a way station on their journey to the Holy Land, it is not surprising that a propagandist (particularly if paid) would base his plea on the same arguments and inducements which had been currently used for years past concerning thirteenth-century crusades. There is no possibility that the so-called *Voie de Tunis* was intended as anything more than the usual banality in favor of an effort which perhaps did not even hold any personal interest for its author.

Further objections to the present interpretation of *Renart le Bestorné* might arise in terms of Rutebeuf's defense of Guillaume de Saint-Amour in the university quarrels of 1250-1257. In defending a close friend against the Mendicant orders, in opposing organizations which counted Thomas Aquinas and Albertus Magnus in their membership, Rutebeuf was manifestly not on the side of those whom to-day one calls the angels. But in any case the forthright poems on the university quarrel were presented without benefit of literary mask, nor did the poet conceal his disagreement with either king or pope. In other words, all the more reason for distinguishing the essential point of *Renart le Bestorné* from mere criticism of the Mendicants.

Thus the veiled language of *Renart le Bestorné* involves something more than the king's crusading enthusiasm and the pope's reluctance to speak his opposition frankly. In the poems on the Mendicants, as in those where the university problem is treated directly, Rutebeuf is acting as a Gallican so far as the ecclesiastical authority is concerned, and that marks an issue where commentators of the day felt free to express their thoughts perfectly openly. But the alleged guilelessness of Louis IX is mentioned in *Renart le Bestorné* and nowhere else in the Rutebeuf repertory (not even in the *Paix de Rutebeuf*, where the court is represented as closed to the poor). It should no longer be hard to imagine why the author of *Renart le Bestorné* resorted to his thinly concealed device of literary mystification.

* * *

Before final review of Rutebeuf's judgement upon Louis IX, it is first needful to paraphrase *Renart le Bestorné* in terms of the interpretations advanced in the preceding pages.

"Corruption can be put down," says Rutebeuf, "from time to time, but never for good. In fact, corruption is right now overrunning France. Like Renart in the old fable, corruption was to have been abolished when the fox was hanged, but actually neither was ever suppressed. I, Rutebeuf, was being naïf when I still thought it could be done.

"Sir Noble, or rather Louis IX, is being run by Renart, whom I identify as Charles of Anjou. The king's brother has gained control over all royal affairs. Charles is agitating for a new crusade and he is scheming to seize the French kingdom in Constantinople, from which Baldwin II has been banished into poverty-stricken exile.

"By stirring up this new crusade, Charles will precipitate a war which France could certainly afford to do without. And the pity is that Louis IX believes that this way lies salvation. He does not realize the intensity of the opposition to this crusade, nor does he know how much he is being criticized in the gossip of Paris and elsewhere. If he did, he would never lend himself to such a project.

"To set aside funds for this crusade, the king has been cutting down on court activities ever since 1261, to such an extent that many deserving individuals are excluded from Hôtel fuctions. In this senseless course he is being abetted not only by Charles of Anjou, but also by such counselors as Jean le Roux of Brittany and Thibaut II of Navarre.

"Louis IX is so guileless in his pietistic and avaricious obstinacy that his bad advisors can with impunity cause endless trouble, while the better elements in the nation must sit by in helpless resignation. The king is so blinded that he has no idea about how pitifully few soldiers he can trust when the time comes for embarking on his crusade.

"If this venture is really undertaken, Charles of Anjou will be leading the way, while the youthful and vainglorious Thibaut will fight the first engagement with the Saracen. Nor will the latter ever thank anyone for good services rendered. Jean of Brittany will doubtless lead the army and, at that, he is likely to run away at the first critical moment. And another 'leader', bearing the great archiepiscopal cross, will surely be the prelate of Rouen, Eudes Rigaud.

"Charles of Anjou and his fellow travelers will be the worst retinue that any king ever had. And they will brook no interference while they manage the affairs of state. Whenever the king offers banquets, they are so bad that everyone leaves. In fact, the royal Hôtel has become such a hermitage that soon nobody will know where the king dwells, because he will obviously be lost in some unknown spot during this insensate crusade.

"The archbishop is mere front while Charles of Anjou handles the financial frauds of the reign. And also, would that Jean of Brittany had to pay dearly for his privilege of carrying the royal seal! These malefactor advisors of Louis IX are truly asking for the gallows. Besides reducing the Hôtel to a hermitage, they are exacting unjust taxes from dioceses as far away as Liège, Metz, Toul, and Verdun. They have brought France to such a sorry state that even an attack by some enemy from the outside would be less disastrous than what we are being forced to put up with now.

"In fact, if king Louis were to come to grief in this newest crusade folly, almost no one would be really sorry for him. So let him go ahead and be as foolish as he likes: I am past caring, just provided that I, Rutebeuf, have no part in the crusade myself."

* * *

Setting aside the possibility that the name "Rutebeuf" was used by more than one versifier (a theory which has been received with rather less than enthusiasm), one finds that the thought content throughout the 56-poem repertory is nowhere profound or obscure. To be sure, there are occasional veiling procedures as in the *Dit des Cordeliers*, in the *Dit de l'Université* (both of which have been admirably clarified by Faral), and in *Renart le Bestorné*, but the particular "message" in each is wholly uninvolved. Much of Rutebeuf's verse is devoted to fun and straight fiction, but he frequently becomes commentator, critic, and pamphleteer. His sensitiveness to injustices and sufferings is always acute and often violent —where these involve other people. Of his own trials and tribulations he speaks in jest: it is highly likely that the vicissitudes he mentions are mainly inventions of a gay imagining, frequently tinged with mock self-pity (cf. *FSpec*, p. 329). Whatever Rutebeuf's station in life, he was clearly no down-trodden nobody: this is shown beyond reasonable doubt by his wide range of literary knowledge and interests, and by his thorough familiarity with politics in court, university, and monastic orders. After all, what other thirteenth-century critic has attacked so many high-placed personages and organizations with explicit excoriation while securing the preservation of his cannonades for posterity?

Rutebeuf's expressed opinions about Louis IX involve the crusading ideal, the banishment of the *maître régent* of the Paris theological faculty, the degeneration of allegedly self-seeking Mendicant orders. These opinions have come to be better and better understood during the last two decades. It is difficult to find in his poems more than perfunctory lip-service in favor of renewed struggles in the Holy Land, whereas there is abundant evidence that Rutebeuf regarded any further crusading in his time as profitless *per se* and also as critically damaging to France. The ardor of his devotion to Guillaume de Saint-Amour and of his disgust with the Mendicant orders has always been recognized with sound unanimity.

The foregoing summary of hints about Rutebeuf's views and emotional outlook includes basic modifications of appraisals which have enjoyed routine acceptance since too many decades ago and which, in some crucial aspects, are still reaffirmed in the Faral-Bastin edition. This observation does not mean, however, that anyone today can claim that everything which has been said hitherto about Rutebeuf's attitude toward Louis IX is inexact: far from it. But, up to now, there has been no real attempt to assemble Rutebeuf's ideas about his king in properly coördinated fashion. Also, these ideas have never been adequately correlated either with Rutebeuf's actual evaluation of crusade projects in the second half of the thirteenth century or with any realistic interest in his still undiscovered position in French society. Indeed, however, the major mystery will always be that his precise feelings and prejudices were not better "explicated" numerous years ago.

At long last, the summary of Louis IX through Rutebeuf's eyes becomes straightforward. First of all, Rutebeuf and Joinville agree about certain of the royal shortcomings, although the author of *Renart le Bestorné* lacks the chronicler's gentle delicacy in foregoing the proffered charms of a crusade destined to founder in the wretched North Africa of 1270. Whereas Joinville, however devoted and kindly, leaves the reader with no doubts about the king's religiously benighted fanaticism, this is something about which Rutebeuf intimates concern only by implication. He nowhere engages in subtleties regarding religious fervor or anything else in that area: his preoccupation is exclusively with the wrongs which he attributes to royal policies and to the counselors who promote them.

Principally, Rutebeuf's grievances against Louis IX are these: (1) misguided zeal for further crusading, but the poet is honest enough to recognize—without reservation—that the king was right in 1261 to remain in France and thereby avert, skilfully, the possible Tartar threat; (2) from 1261 on, Louis IX was unjust to subjects of merit when he denied them continuing privileges in the royal Hôtel; (3) Louis IX was an outright deceiver when he promised Guillaume de Saint-Amour the fair hearing which was never allowed to take place; (4) the king was forever letting himself be gulled by Mendicant and other sycophants; (5) Louis IX crusaded at the wrong time when he brought upon himself the disaster of 1248-1254. It is clear that, as Rutebeuf judged the political situation during the final two decades of the reign, Louis IX impressed him as a credulous fanatic in terms of crusades and religion, and also as a ruler with the kind of dictatorial arrogance which was successfully played upon by the venal self-servers whom he so unwittingly admitted into his intimate counsel.

Concerning the three years between the 1267 crusade commitment and the king's death in Tunis, Joinville has proved himself lastingly justified. Although without the chronicler's relative calm, has Rutebeuf done less?

After seven printings (cf. *FB* I, p. 537) of *Renart le Bestorné*, it may seem odd that an eighth is offered here. Until now, however, the poem has remained sufficiently controversial, both on editorial and on interpretive grounds, to call for a final textual attempt. Since matters of historical import have been treated in the preceding pages, this chapter is also intended to serve as convenient reference concerning Rutebeuf and Louis IX.

Renart le Bestorné is preserved in three manuscripts, all in the *fonds français* of the Bibliothèque Nationale: 837 (A), 1593 (B), 1635 (C). Thus far, the only editions of consequence by other investigators (Jubinal, Faral) are based on A, but it has been correctly recognized that textually the version in C has at least parallel claims to authenticity. In fact, in *Neuphilologische Mitteilungen* (LIII [1952], p. 119), Artur Långfors prefers C, although his observations are confined to the textual picture in Rutebeuf's *Vie de sainte Marie l'Egyptienne*. For *Renart le Bestorné* as presented here, C is selected as basic manuscript. For variants from A and from the mediocre B, see *FB* I, pp. 537-544. Emendations of C, and the occasional errors in *FB*, are indicated in the notes (*infra*) which follow the translation of the poem. Several passages in this translation adapt borrowings from Faral and from Fay (*RPh* I, p. 164) which have been gladly appropriated.

* * *

Ci encoumence li diz de Renart le Bestornei

Renars est mors, Renars est vis,
Renars est ors, Renars est vilz,

Et Renars reingne.
Renars at moult reinei el reingne;
Bien i chevauche a lasche reigne,
    Coul estendu.
Hon le devoit avoir pendu
Si com je l'avoie entendu,
    Mais non at voir:
Par tanz le porreiz bien veoir.
Il est sires de tout l'avoir
    Mon seigneur Noble
Et de la Brie et dou Vignoble.
Renars fist en Coustantinoble
    Bien ces aviaux,
Et en cazes et en caviaux
Ne laissat vaillant .ij. naviaux
    L'empereour,
Ainz en fist povre pescheour;
Par pou ne le fist pescheour
    Dedens la meir.
Ne doit hon bien Renart ameir,
Qu'en Renart n'at fors que l'ammeir,
    C'est sa droiture.
Renars at mout grant norreture,
Mout en avons de sa nature
    En ceste terre.
Renars porra mouvoir teil gueirre
Dont mout bien se porroit sosferre
    La regions.
Mes sires Nobles li lyons
Cuide que sa sauvacions
    De Renart vaigne:
Non fait voir — de Dieu li sovaingne.
Ansois dout qu'il ne l'en aveingne
    Damage et honte.
Se Nobles savoit que ce monte
Et les paroles que om conte
    Par mi la vile, —
Dame Raimbors, dame Poufille,
Qui de lui tiennent lor concile,

         Sa .x., sa vint,
Et dïent c'onques mais n'avint
N'onques a franc cuer ne souvint
         De teil gieu faire!
Bien li deüst membreir de Daire
Que li sien firent a mort traire
         Par s'avarice.
Quant j'oi parleir de si grant vice,
Par foi toz li peuz m'en herice
         De duel et d'ire
Si fort que je ne sai que dire,
Car je voi roiaume et empire
         Trestout encemble.
Que dites vos? Que vos en semble
Quant mes sires Nobles dessemble
         Toutes ces bestes
Qu'il ne pueent metre lor testes
A boens jors ne a bones festes
         En sa maison?
Et se n'i seit nule raison
Fors qu'il doute de la saison
         Qu'i n'encherisse.
Mais jai de ceste annee n'isse
Ne mais coustume n'estaublisse
         Qui se brassa!
Car trop vilain fait embrassa:
Roniaux li chiens le porchassa
         Avec Renart.
Nobles ne seit enging ne art
Nes c'uns des asnes de Senart
         Qui buche porte;
Il ne seit pas de qu'est sa porte,
Por ce fait mal qui li ennorte
         Se tout bien non.
Des bestes orrois ci le non
Qui de mal faire ont le renon
         Touz jors eü.
Moult ont grevei, moult ont neü;
Au seigneurs en est mescheü

>   Et il s'en passent.
> Asseiz emblent, asseiz amassent,
> C'est merveilles qu'il ne se lassent.
>   Or entendeiz   84
> Com Nobles at les yeux bandeiz.
> Et ce ces oz estoit mandeiz
>   Par bois, par terre,
> Ou porroit il troveir ne querre   88
> En cui il se fiast de guerre,
>   Ce mestiers iere?
> Renars porteroit la baniere,
> Roniaus qu'a toz fait laide chiere   92
> Feroit la bataille premiere
>   O soi nelui.
> Bien vos puis dire de celui
> Ja nuns n'avra honeur de lui   96
>   De par servise.
> Quant la choze seroit emprise,
> Ysangrins que chacuns desprise
>   L'ost conduroit   100
> Ou, se devient, il s'en furoit.
> Bernars l'asnes les deduroit
>   A tout sa crois.
> Cist quatre sont fontainne et doix,   104
> Cist quatre ont l'otroi et la voix
>   De tout l'ostei.
> La choze gist en teil costei
> Que rois de bestes ne l'ot teil —   108
>   Le bel aroi!
> Se sunt bien maignie de roi,
> Il n'aimment noise ne desroi
>   Ne grant murmure.   112
> Quant mes sires Nobles pasture,
> Chacuns s'en ist de la pasture,
>   Nuns n'i remaint.
> Par tanz ne savrons ou il maint.   116
> Ja autrement ne se demaint
>   Por faire avoir,
> Qu'il en devra asseiz avoir

Et cil ont asseiz de savoir
    Qui font son conte.
Bernars gete, Renars mesconte,
Ne connoissent honeur de honte.
    Roniaus abaie
Et Ysengrins pas ne s'esmaie,
Le seel porte; tpropt que il paie!
    Gart chacuns soi!
Ysangrins at .i. fil o soi
Qui toz jors de mal faire a soi,
    S'a non Primaut;
Renars .i. qui at non Grimaut;
Poi lor est coument ma rime aut
    Mais que mal fassent
Et que toz les bons us effacent.
Diex lor otroit ce qu'il porchacent,
    S'avront la corde.
Lor ouvragne bien c'i acorde,
Car il sunt sens misericorde
    Et sens pitié,
Sens charitei, sans amistié.
Mon seigneur Noble ont tot gitié
    De boens usages,
Ses hosteiz est .i. rencluzages.
Asseiz font paier de muzages
    Et d'avaloignes
A ces povres bestes lontoingnes
A cui il font de grans essoingnes.
    Diex les confonde
Qui sires est de tot le monde,
Et je rostroi que l'en me tonde
    Se maux n'en vient,
Car d'un proverbe me sovient
Que hon dit tot pert qui tot tient;
    C'est a boen droit.
La choze gist en teil endroit
Que chacune beste vorroit
    Que venist l'once.
Se Nobles çopoit a la ronce,

De mil n'est pas .i. qui en gronce ; 159
    C'est voirs cens faille.
Hom senege guerre et bataille,
Il ne m'en chaut mais que bien n'aille. 162

EXPLICIT

* * *

Ici commence le "dit" de Renart le bétourné.

(Vv. 1-6) Renart est mort, Renart est en vie ; Renart est sale, Renart est ignoble ; et Renart règne. Il y a longtemps que Renart a la haute main sur le royaume ; il y fait force chevauchées à bride avalée, le cou raidi.

(7-13) Il avait été destiné au gibet, d'après ce qu'on m'avait fait accroire, mais il n'en est rien ; avec le temps vous aurez l'occasion de vous en rendre pleinement compte. C'est lui le maître de tous les biens de messire Noble, y compris la Brie et le Vignoble.

(14-21) A Constantinople, Renart réalisa toutes ses ambitions, car, ni dans les maisons ni aux caves, il ne laissa à l'empereur pour deux navets : au contraire, Renart fit de lui un pauvre pécheur, et peu s'en fallut qu'il n'en fit un [simple] pêcheur en mer.

(22-27) Comme tout chez Renart n'est rien moins qu'amer, chacun doit l'avoir en haine ; c'est ce qu'il mérite. Renart s'est multiplié d'une grande engeance ; et de cet acabit, nous avons bien notre quote-part dans ce pays.

(28-36) Renart sera en état de faire déclencher une guerre si affreuse que le pays pourrait bien s'en dispenser. Messire Noble le lion croit que son salut éternel relève de Renart, mais la chose n'en est certainement pas ainsi ; que le roi se souvienne de Dieu ! Or, puisse-t-il plutôt redouter que malheur et honte n'en viennent l'accabler.

(37-45) Si Noble savait réellement à quoi s'en tenir ! si seulement il était au fait des propos qui circulent partout dans la ville ! s'il pouvait apprendre que telle dame Raimbourc et telle dame Poufile — sans compter des dizaines de commères par ici, des vingtaines par là — passent leur temps à s'entretenir de ses affaires et à se répéter que jamais auparavant il n'est ni survenu ni arrivé à noble coeur de se prêter à jeu pareil!

(46-54) Noble devrait bien se souvenir de Darius, dont l'avarice lui valut d'être mis à mort par ses propres hommes. Cela me fait dresser les cheveux rien que d'entendre parler d'un si grand vice; j'en éprouve une douleur et un chagrin si vifs que je ne sais que dire, car je vois confondus royaume et empire, [s'empirant] tous deux à la fois.

(55-63) Qu'en dites-vous? Et, du moment que messire Noble chasse toutes ses bêtes tant et si bien qu'elles ne peuvent se montrer dans sa maison ni lors des festins publics ni aux jours de fête, quelle idée enfin vous en faites-vous? Et à ce propos, pourtant, Noble ne connaît aucune raison, si ce n'est sa crainte que les temps ne deviennent durs.

(64-69) Mais celui qui brassa tout cela a embrassé une bien vilaine politique; qu'il meure donc avant la fin de cette année sans jamais instituer une seule coutume [royale] de plus! C'est avec Renart que le chien Roniel a machiné [ces mesures de restriction].

(70-75) Quant à l'artifice ou à la ruse, Noble n'en sait pas plus long qu'un de ces ânes de Senart qui portent des bûches; il n'entend rien à sa charge [de roi], d'où il s'ensuit que celui qui l'exhorte agit mal, à moins [évidemment] qu'il ne lui profère de bons conseils.

(76-83) Vous entendrez nommer ici les bêtes qui de tout temps doivent leurs réputations au mal qu'elles font. Elles ont combiné bien des oppressions, elles ont répandu bien des malheurs. Les [bons] seigneurs en ont beaucoup souffert, alors que les malfaiteurs sont indifférents; ceux-ci font beaucoup d'escroqueries et amassent des richesses; on s'étonne qu'ils ne se lassent pas.

(84-89) Or écoutez, [si vous voulez savoir] comment Noble a les yeux bandés. Et si, d'un bout à l'autre des bois et du pays, son armée était sommée de se réunir, où pourrait-il trouver ou chercher à qui se fier en cas de guerre?

(90-94) Ce serait, au besoin, Renart qui porterait la bannière; Roniel, qui fait grise mine à tout le monde, formerait à lui tout seul le premier corps de troupes.

(95-103) De celui-ci je puis bien vous dire que jamais personne n'aura de lui la récompense d'un service. [Bien que] méprisé de tous, Ysengrin conduirait l'armée quand le combat s'engagerait, ou bien il pourrait s'enfuir; et l'âne Bernart marcherait en avant, avec sa croix.

(104-109) Ces quatre sont et fontaine et source [i. e., c'est d'eux que tout dépend], et l'Hôtel tout entier est soumis à leurs voix et autorité. Les choses en sont au point que jamais roi de bêtes n'a eu cour pareille — la belle équipe!

(110-115) C'est une fameuse maisonnée de roi que ces animaux-là! Ils n'aiment ni tracas ni désordre ni grands murmures. Quand messire Noble "pâture", chaque bête quitte le "pâturage" [c'est-à-dire, la table du roi]; aucun n'y reste.

(116-121) Après quelque temps nous ne saurons plus où retrouver son gîte. Qu'il ne se démène jamais de façon différente pour augmenter ses biens, parce qu'il devra en avoir largement assez et que les comptables qui s'occupent de ses finances sont singulièrement avertis.

(122-127) Bernart établit les comptes, Renart les fausse; ni l'un ni l'autre ne savent distinguer honneur de honte. Roniel aboie et Ysengrin ne s'effraie de rien; le loup porte le sceau — que ce fût bien lui qui paie! Que chacun s'en garde!

(128-134) Ysengrin a avec lui un fils Primaut qui a toujours soif de faire du mal; [de même] Renart en a un qui s'appelle Grimaut. Peu leur importe l'allure de mes rimes, pourvu qu'ils soient libres de se vouer au mal et qu'ils parviennent à enrayer toutes les bonnes institutions.

(135-140) Que Dieu leur accorde ce qu'ils recherchent, et si bien qu'ils auront la potence! Leurs activités cadrent à merveille avec cette perspective, car ils sont sans miséricorde et sans pitié, sans charité, sans amitié.

(141-147) Ils ont détourné messire Noble si complètement des bons usages que son Hôtel est devenu un hermitage. Ils font payer beaucoup de débauches et de bagatelles par ces malheureuses bêtes lointaines, auxquelles ils causent en effet de grands ennuis.

(148-154) Que Dieu le Seigneur du monde entier les confonde! Et moi, à mon tour, je veux bien qu'on me tonde si le mal qu'ils font ne retombe pas sur eux, car par ouï-dire je me rappelle le proverbe "qui trop embrasse mal étreint"; ce qui est parfaitement juste.

(155-162) Les choses en sont au point que chaque bête voudrait que l'once vînt [sévir]. Si Noble devait trébucher sur les ronces, il n'y aurait pas un sur mille pour protester ; c'est là la vérité, et sans faute. Que l'on présage guerre et bataille ; je ne m'en soucie pas, pourvu que je n'y prenne part moi-même.

* * *

TEXTUAL NOTES

1-21. For reminiscences from the *Roman de Renart*, see *FRom*, p. 258, and *FB* I, pp. 537-538.

4. The C reading, *et* as against A *el* and B *ou*, is admissible but probably not authentic.

5-6. From these verses Leo infers (p. 112) an "unusual rage, a nervous heat, in which [the poet] sees images which are directly and fearsomely comprehensible, images which perhaps affect the dreamer elsewhere as burdens on his mind or just as mere nightmares: this agitation, this disturbance in his innermost being, regardless of the occasion, was indeed Rutebeuf's most forthright and most innate talent, and, in my opinion, the one which most essentially distinguishes him from his versifying contemporaries".

7. Faral translates: "on prétendait qu'il avait été pendu".

10. AB read *savoir*, against C *veoir*. The manifest frequency of leonine rhyme in *Renart le Bestorné* virtually requires adherence to AB in the edited text.

11-12. Leo claims (p. 76) that the parallel with vv. 148-149 is not a mere accident of style, but rather a deliberate device on the part of the author to recall that "God, the ruler of the world, is still more powerful than Renart, the ruler of France".

13. In his *FB* note to this verse, as previously in *FRom* (p. 258), Faral maintains that, since *vignoble* is a common noun, *Brie* must be likewise. Why so, necessarily? The two passages which he cites in order to suggest that *brie* may mean "city" are in no way conclusive. To imply that Renart has gained mastery of "city and vineyard" clarifies nothing. But the two questions remain: why Brie and what vineyard? Faral has no comment about Tiburtius Denkinger's suggestion (*Franziskanische Studien* II [1915], p. 102) that *vignoble* might designate the Lord's vineyard: that is, the Church. In v. 71 Rutebeuf mentions the forest of Senart, which happens to be situated in Brie: could there be a connection? Faral points out that Brie was not in the royal domain, yet since 1259 it was among the "fiefs mouvant de la couronne". Rutebeuf had his own good reason (if perhaps only for needs of *-oble* rhyme) for placing *Brie* and *vignoble* in juxtaposition: the fact that no one to-day has determined that reason discounts any certainty that *Brie*-*brie* is a common noun.

14-21. Faral is of course correct (*FRom*, p. 258) in remarking that at this point Rutebeuf is "encore dans la fiction du *Roman de Renart*, branche XI, où Noble est empereur et où sa capitale est Constantinople", from which, however, Noble in the animal fable is not dislodged. In *Renart le Bestorné*, on the other hand, the emperor's discomfiture is total. So also was that of

Baldwin II, driven from Constantinople in 1261 and further displaced by Charles of Anjou when the Treaty of Viterbo was concluded in 1267, yet Faral states categorically that "ici il n'y a aucun renvoi à l'histoire". Whether Rutebeuf wrote his poem early or late in the 1260's, it is inconceivable that he was unaware of the fall of the Latin kingdom of Constantinople. It seems self-evident that in this passage Rutebeuf is thinking of Baldwin II and of Branch XI, both. Excellent further confirmation has recently been provided by Alfred L. Foulet (*FSpec*, p. 331).

17. Faral's reading *laissa* is an error for the *lessa* in manuscript A.

24. Faral interprets *sa droiture* as "sa règle, son propre".

28. In 1948 Faral suggested (*FRom*, p. 258) that *gueirre* may refer either to internal strife or to hostilities from outside, but found it difficult to decide which. In the edition, however, he says that "il n'y a aucune raison de penser (malgré le v. 161) qu'il s'agisse de guerre extérieure": he finds it more reasonable to equate *gueirre* with the "désordres intérieurs que pourraient créer Renart et ses suppôts" (cf. *FSpec*, p. 330). His note on v. 28 offers no supporting reason for this view. In the edition, moreover, Faral drops his earlier reference to the *Complainte de Constantinople* (vv. 154-156), where Rutebeuf is explicitly concerned over a threat of invasion from without.

32. Faral agrees (*FRom*, p. 258) that *sauvacions* is a religious term involving the idea of spiritual salvation. But in the edition he sees vv. 31-33 as a probable allusion to the king's trust in the Mendicants, *sauvacions* "pouvant s'entendre soit au sens matériel, soit au sens religieux".

34. In manuscript C the first word in the verse is clearly *Nou*.

35. As Faral points out in *FB*, *dout* can mean either "je crains" or "qu'il craigne", but in *FRom* he preferred the latter. In a further reference to this line (*FB* I, p. 216) *aviegne* from A is incorrectly replaced by *soviegne*.

37-45. For the syntax, cf. the *FB* notes on vv. 93-104 of the *Dit de Guillaume de Saint-Amour* and on vv. 109-111 of the *Dit de Sainte Eglise*.

38. The A reading *l'en* avoids the *que om* hiatus in C.

40. While Poufille is mentioned in the *Roman de Renart* (Branch Va, v. 1147: cf. Leo, p. 55), Raimbors, so far as I know, does not appear in the beast epic. Leo recalls the diatribe of Sarette de Faillouel against Louis IX, as recorded by Guillaume de Saint-Pathus (ed. H.-F. Delaborde, pp. 118-119). This outburst resembles those in the exemplum of Trajan and the widow (cf. Gaston Paris, *Bibliothèque de l'Ecole des Hautes Etudes* XXXV [1878], pp. 261-298) and in that of the old woman and the tyrant (cf. Johannes Bolte, *Kleinere Schriften zur erzählenden Dichtung des Mittelalters von Reinhold Köhler*, II [Berlin, 1900], pp. 362-363).

46. Only manuscripts CA include *de*.

55. C reads *vos*, not *vous* (as in the *FB* variant).

56-60. For Leo (p. 56) this passage is a pivotal point in the poem and he infers, gratuitously, that Rutebeuf himself had been expelled from the court (cf. also pp. 70 and 94). Leo describes the poet's view of Louis IX as follows (p. 57): "It had really happened, and it was evident to all, that a pious, modest and prudent man had succeeded to the French throne, and that his entire attention, guided by the achievements of his predecessors, was directed by diplomacy and good will, as well as by indulgence and steadfastness, toward suppression of the gay yet undisciplined feudal aristocracy and toward development of the beginnings of a solid bourgeoisie. However, he also inclined more than was desirable to preconceived notions, to pietism, and — in private and public appearances — to a kind of respectability bordering on philistinism. The king was a man who preferred to be attended and advised by learned clear-thinking monks and bourgeois officials — and yet likewise by ecclesiastical hypocrites — rather than by princes proud of their lineage or by illiterate knights, not to mention free-thinking progressives. In this way, to be sure, his court could still have more in common with a cloister than with an old-style northern feudal court or than with a meridional court of love, such as the one from which his young queen Marguerite had been cut adrift." Leo concludes, therefore, that *Renart le Bestorné* was motivated by Rutebeuf's supposed expulsion from the royal entourage and by the more basic attitude just summarized.

61. The B variant in *FB* should read *Et si ny*.

62-63. For other examples of prolepsis in Rutebeuf, see *FB* I, p. 199. For *qu'i* (= *qu'il*) 63, Faral prefers either the *que* of A or the *quel* (= *qu'el*) of B. In C the subject of *encherisse* is of course impersonal. In *FB* the B variant (v. 62) should read *il redoubte la*.

68. C reads *la* instead of *le*.

71. *Senart* may have been introduced simply to ease a rhyming situation, but it may also be local coloring indicative of the author's acquaintance with (or even provenience from?) the Corbeil region of Brie, south of Paris. Faral grants (*FRom*, p. 260) that "Rutebeuf connaissait la région, mais n'en était pas originaire". However, there is no categoric evidence either for or against the latter part of his assertion.

73. Faral discusses *porte* at some length (*FRom*, p. 260, and *FB* I, p. 541). Literally, the word may mean "gate" (hence figuratively, "course"?) or, perhaps, "portage". The latter possibility, as Faral notes, gains some support from a passage cited in Godefroy VI, 314a. In any case, the contextual intent of the verse is clear.

80. The *FB* text reads *Aus seignors,* which according to manuscript A is correct. B reads *Au seigneur* (with *ur* in superscript abbreviation). Although Faral recognizes that *au* for *aus* is frequent in C, he takes this thirteenth-century inflexional situation sufficiently seriously here to say that "on ne sait donc s'il s'agit du roi ou des seigneurs"! Cf. *FSpec*, p. 331.

82. *FB*, editing from A, should read *emblent* rather than *amblent*.

85. *FB*, editing from A, should read *bendez*, rather than *bandez*.

86-90. For the syntax, cf. *FB* I, p. 169. Changing his opinion since *FRom*, Faral has decided correctly that v. 90 belongs in this passage, rather than with the verses which follow.

91-93. The metrical system in the poem indicates that one of these lines should not have been in the original. On the other hand, vv. 104-105 require that all four animals mentioned in vv. 91-103 be accounted for in the course of this passage. Furthermore, each of the three manuscripts gives vv. 91-93. Possibly a common source of all three versions omitted a few verses at about this point, where further comment on Renart might have been intended by the author. Against this last suggestion, of course, is the fact that vv. 91-93 have the same rhyme. Just possibly, instead of vv. 92-93 as transmitted in the manuscripts, Rutebeuf may have written nothing more than *Roniaus la bataille premiere*. Faral offers no comment.

102. Two errors in Faral's transcript from A, which reads *Bernart* and *deduiroit* (the latter is mispelled again in the *FB* glossary). In *FB* why include the merely orthographic variant *deduroit* from C?

104-105. In these lines, the *quatre* of C is spelled out in the manuscript: the roman numerals noted in the *FB* variants appear only in **AB**.

107-109. Manuscript C reads *ceil* instead of *teil* 107. The *FB* note to vv. 107-109 brings confusion to a passage which raises no notable difficulty in any of the mediaeval versions. Why does Faral no longer regard v. 109 as independent (cf. *FRom*, p. 260)?

111-112. Faral's note: "C'est-à-dire: ou bien qu'ils n'aiment pas voir trop de monde à la cour, ou bien qu'ils opèrent en catimini."

113-118. Cf. *Mariage de Rutebeuf*, vv. 99-103: *L'en ne savra ja ou je mains / Por ma poverte; / Ja n'i sera ma porte ouverte, / Quar ma meson est trop deserte / Et povre et gaste.*

120. Ewert agrees (*Medium Aevum* XVII [1948], p. 54) that the reading of AB is superior to the *Cil seivent asseiz savoir* of manuscript C.

121. The B variant in *FB* should be deleted.

122. In *FB* Faral states that *gete* means "tient les écritures et, spécialement, fixe des impôts". His explanation in *FRom*, accepted in the translation here, seems slightly more judicious.

123. *FB* should have included the B variant, *ne* for *de*.

126. Despite a number of examples in Godefroy (VIII, 93c), the precise meaning of *tpropt* remains elusive. For two of the examples, Godefroy regards it as an interjection of indignation or scorn; for the others, as one of encouragement. In the glossary for Jean Bodel's *Jeu de saint Nicolas*, Jeanroy specifies that it ordinarily means "vite!" or "hors d'ici!". In the glossary for *Deux Miracles de Sainte Vierge par Gautier de Coinci* (Uppsala, 1955), Erik Rankka has "pet, interjection d'indignation ou de mépris: fi! pouah!" (cf. also his note, p. 167). In a note on v. 90 of Rutebeuf's *Des Règles*, *FB* takes *tpropt* as a "bravade, faisant penser à une inconvenance", but in the glossary Mlle Bastin calls it simply an interjection of encouragement, and cites this verse of *Renart le Bestorné*, where it most certainly implies impatience mingled with disgust. Also, as in *FRom*, Faral edits *tpropt que il paie* as a quotation, because "ce sont des paroles à mettre dans la bouche d'Isengrin, qui fait payer": this is possible, but scarcely likely. — Lastly, v. 126 is hypermetric in C, but it seems hardly useful to emend *que il* to *qu'il*.

129. In the *FB* recording of the B variant there should be no punctuation after *a*.

131. The comma after *un* in the *FB* text is unnecessary.

134. Faral's text should read *esfacent* instead of *effacent*.

136. Except for an unimportant reservation, Leo accepts (pp. 75, 104) Denkinger's elaborately argued theory that this verse gives a pun on the word *corde* (*Franziskanische Studien* II [1915], pp. 99-100), which might possibly mean the Franciscan loin-girdle as well as the gallows rope. It is, however, no longer necessary or constructive to attempt to read so much into this single word.

137. *Ouurage*, the B variant for *ouvragne*, is not recorded in *FB*.

141. Instead of *tot*, A reads *tuit* which in *FB* (I, p. 158) is regarded as an adjective with adverbial value. It is simpler to treat the spelling in A as scribal carelessness.

144. Faral explains *paier de muzages* (agreeing with Leo before him, p. 75 [note 58a] as "payer (à son détriment) le prix d'un temps perdu, ne rien obtenir", but Mlle Bastin glosses *muzages* as "frais du jeu".

145. Only this occurrence of *avaloignes* is recorded in Tobler-Lommatzsch, but without any translation. Godefroy, reading *analoignes* (I, 282a), suggests "chicanes, longueurs, délais, p.-ê. le même mot qu'*aloigne*". Under the entry **abellanea* (modern *aveline*), von Wartburg notes that *aviloignes* is attested in fourteenth-century Burgundian, but it is difficult to see the relevance of filberts in *Renart le Bestorné* except as possibly figurative for something like bagatelles. Cf. also E. Philipon, *Romania* XXXIX (1910), p. 508

147. *FB* glosses *essoingnes* as "difficultés, embarras". Presumably the word refers to specific exactions prior to the 1270 crusade. "Les Eglises de Liège, de Metz, de Toul et de Verdun, quoique étrangères au royaume, étaient soumises à la même taxe" (H.-A. Wallon, *Saint Louis et son temps*, II [Paris, 1876], p. 427).

157. As Richard T. Holbrook has pointed out (*Dante and the animal kingdom* [New York, 1902], p. 93), the pard, and therefore the ounce, might be identified with the Antichrist, a solution which would make sense in *Renart le Bestorné*. So also would Faral's suggestion that, by way of Branch I*b* (v. 2828) of the *Roman de Renart*, the ounce recalls the first beast of the *Apocalypse* (ch. 13). Cf. also Leo, pp. 77-81; Pliny the Elder, *Naturalis Historia*, VIII, 21-25 (ed. H. Rackham [Loeb Classical Library, 1940], vol. III, pp. 44-49); Gerónimo Gómez de Huerta, *Tradución de los Libros de Caio Plinio Segundo, de la historia natural de los animales* (Alcalá, 1602), Libro VIII, ff. 157r° — 160v°.

162. Faral rejects the translation "pourvu que" for *mais que* and proposes that this verse means "peu m'importe désormais que les choses aillent mal". Manuscript A reads *Il ne me chaut*, without the *en* which appears in CB. Faral suggests that *en* may refer, not to what precedes, but to what will follow: because, if it refers to the thought in v. 161, then v. 162 in C would mean "peu m'importe pourvu que les choses aillent mal" which, he comments, would be a "voeu monstrueux". In this connection, it is recalled that Fay has asked (*RPh* I, p. 164) if *mais que bien n'aille* "might not be a malevolent final shaft: 'but I hope it goes badly'". Syntactically, either of Faral's suggestions is quite as possible as the one in the translation which precedes these notes. The latter is ruled out, Faral says (*FRom*, p. 262), by the word *bien*: why? Furthermore, he adds, it would never have occurred to anyone that Rutebeuf might go to war himself: why not? — In the *Complainte de Constantinople* Rutebeuf calls on God to protect cities in the Holy Land, adding that he can give them no other help, because *je ne sui mes hom de guerre* (v. 30). This renders only the more plausible the view that *Renart le Bestorné* concludes on an equally personal note, especially given the presence of *me* in its closing line.

Explicit. — The *u* in *bestourné* is not in A.

ABREVIATIONS

FB. *Oeuvres complètes de Rutebeuf,* publiées par Edmond Faral et Julia Bastin (2 vols.: Paris, 1959-1960).

FRom. Edmond Faral, *Romania* LXX (1948), pp. 257-269.

FSpec. Alfred L. Foulet, *Speculum* XXXVI (1961), pp. 328-332. Review of *FB*.

Leo. Ulrich Leo, "Studien zu Rutebeuf: Entwicklungsgeschichte und Form des *Renart le Bestorné* und der ethisch-politischen Dichtungen Rutebeufs", *Zeitschrift für Romanische Philologie,* Beiheft 67 (Halle, 1922).

PC. *Onze Poèmes de Rutebeuf concernant la croisade,* publiés par Julia Bastin et Edmond Faral (Paris, 1946).

RPh. *Romance Philology* (University of California, 1947-).

www.ingramcontent.com/pod-product-compliance
Lightning Source LLC
Chambersburg PA
CBHW021848220426
43663CB00005B/454